This Book Belongs To:

____

VILLAGE JOURNALS &
NOTEBOOKS
... it takes a village ...

Copyright 2019 – Village Journals & Notebook
All rights reserved

Believe that anything is possible.

Believe you can do it.

You become what you believe.

Believe in yourself. Go after your dreams.

Believe that anything is possible.

Believe you can do it.

You become what you believe.

Believe in yourself. Go after your dreams.

Believe that anything is possible.

Believe you can do it.

Believe in yourself. Go after your dreams.

Believe that anything is possible.

Believe you can do it.

You become what you believe.

Believe in yourself. Go after your dreams.

Believe that anything is possible.

Believe you can do it.

You become what you believe.

Believe you can do it.

You become what you believe.

Believe in yourself. Go after your dreams.

Believe that anything is possible.

Believe you can do it.

You become what you believe.

Believe in yourself. Go after your dreams.

Believe that anything is possible.

Believe you can do it.

You become what you believe.

Believe that anything is possible.

Believe you can do it.

Believe in yourself. Go after your dreams.

Believe that anything is possible.

You become what you believe.

Believe that anything is possible.

Believe you can do it.

You become what you believe.

Believe in yourself. Go after your dreams.

Believe that anything is possible.

Believe you can do it.

You become what you believe.

Believe in yourself. Go after your dreams.

Believe that anything is possible.

You become what you believe.

Believe in yourself. Go after your dreams.

Believe that anything is possible.

You become what you believe.

Believe in yourself. Go after your dreams.

Believe that anything is possible.

You become what you believe.

Believe in yourself. Go after your dreams.

Believe that anything is possible.

Believe you can do it.

You become what you believe.

Believe in yourself. Go after your dreams.

Believe that anything is possible.

Believe you can do it.

You become what you believe.

Believe in yourself. Go after your dreams.

Believe that anything is possible.

Believe you can do it.

You become what you believe.

Believe in yourself. Go after your dreams.

Believe that anything is possible.

Believe you can do it.

You become what you believe.

Believe in yourself. Go after your dreams.

Believe that anything is possible.

Believe you can do it.

You become what you believe.

Believe that anything is possible.

Believe you can do it.

You become what you believe.

Believe that anything is possible.

Believe you can do it.

You become what you believe.

Believe in yourself. Go after your dreams.

Believe that anything is possible.

Believe you can do it.

You become what you believe.

Believe in yourself. Go after your dreams.

Believe that anything is possible.

Believe you can do it.

You become what you believe.

Believe in yourself. Go after your dreams.

Believe that anything is possible.

Believe you can do it.

You become what you believe.

Believe in yourself. Go after your dreams.

Believe that anything is possible.

Believe you can do it.

You become what you believe.

VILLAGE JOURNALS &
NOTEBOOKS

... it takes a village ...

Visit our author page on Amazon to see our complete
collection of books.

www.amazon.com/author/village-journals-notebooks

www.ingramcontent.com/pod-product-compliance
Lightning Source LLC
Chambersburg PA
CBHW061403250726
48657CB00004B/1633